BEGINNING PIANO SOLO

CARTOON Favorites

T0081649

ISBN 978-1-5400-3096-2

Hal•Leonard®

For all works contained herein:
Unauthorized copying, arranging, adapting, recording, Internet posting, public performance,
or other distribution of the music in this publication is an infringement of copyright.
Infringers are liable under the law.

Visit Hal Leonard Online at
www.halleonard.com

Contact Us:
Hal Leonard
7777 West Bluemound Road
Milwaukee, WI 53213
Email: info@halleonard.com

In Europe contact:
Hal Leonard Europe Limited
42 Wigmore Street
Marylebone, London, W1U 2RN
Email: info@halleonardeurope.com

In Australia contact:
Hal Leonard Australia Pty. Ltd.
4 Lentara Court
Cheltenham, Victoria, 3192 Australia
Email: info@halleonard.com.au

BATMAN: The Animated Series

(Main Title)

from BATMAN: The Animated Series

By DANNY ELFMAN

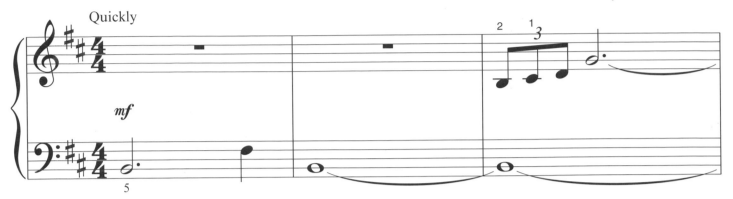

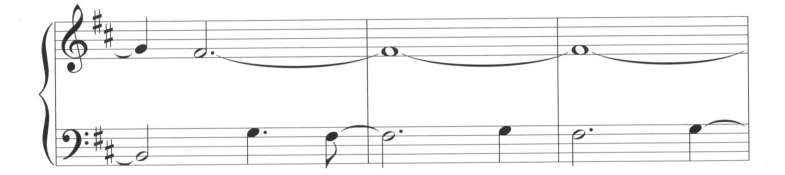

BOB THE BUILDER
(Main Title)

Words and Music by
PAUL K. JOYCE

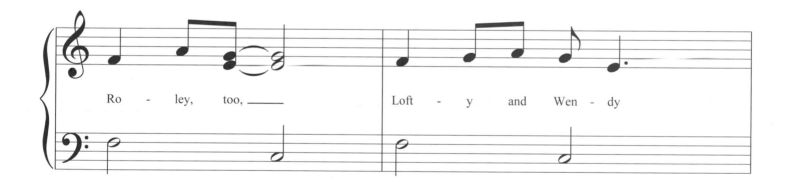

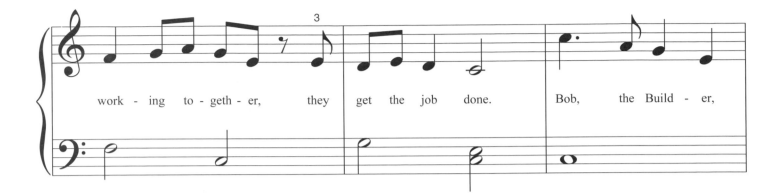

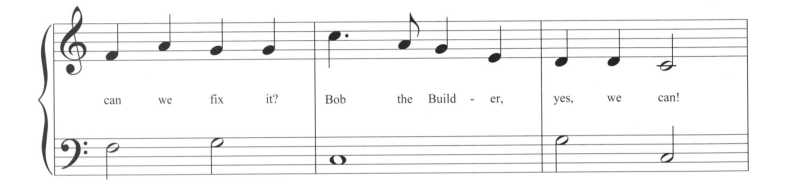

working - ing to - geth - er, they get the job done.

Can we build it? Yeah! Can we

fix it? Yeah! Bob, the Build - er, can we fix it?

Bob the Build - er, yes, we can! _____

LINUS AND LUCY

from A CHARLIE BROWN CHRISTMAS

By VINCE GUARALDI

Moderately

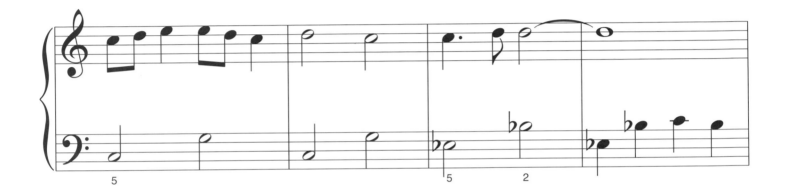

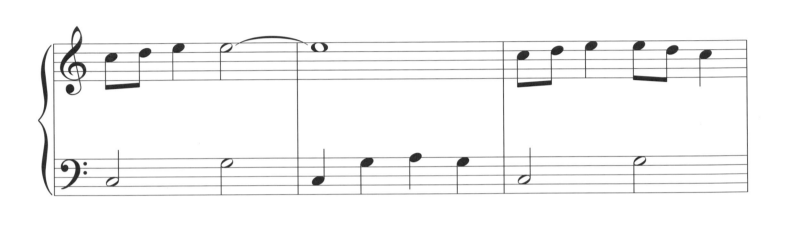

PAW PATROL THEME

Words and Music by JEFF COHEN,
MOLLY KAYE, SCOTT KRIPPAYNE
and MICHAEL "SMIDI" SMITH

14

job's too big! No pup's too small! PAW Pa - trol! We're

on a roll! _____ So here we go! PAW Pa - trol!

Whoa, oh, oh! PAW Pa - trol! Whoa, oh,

oh, oh! PAW Pa - trol! *(Ruff!)*

THEME FROM SPIDER MAN

Written by BOB HARRIS
and PAUL FRANCIS WEBSTER

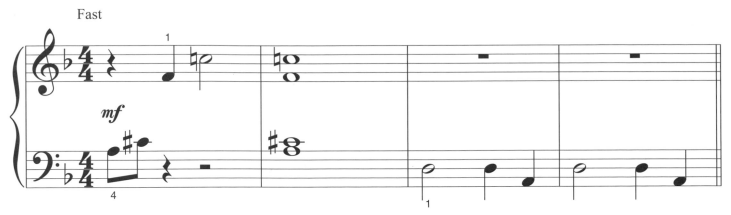

Spi - der Man, ___ Spi - der Man, ___ does what - ev - er a
Is he strong? ___ Lis - ten, bud; ___ he's got ra - di - o -

spi - der can. ___ Spins a web ___ an - y size, ___
ac - tive blood. ___ Can he swing ___ from a thread? ___

catch - es thieves ___ just like flies. ___ Look out!
Take a look ___ o - ver - head. ___ Hey there!

Here comes the Spi - der Man.
There goes the Spi - der Man.

In the chill of night, at the scene of a crime, —

— like a streak of light, he ar - rives just in time! —

— Spi - der Man, — Spi - der Man, — friend - ly neigh - bor - hood

Spi - der Man. ___ Wealth and fame, ___ he's ig - nored. ___

Ac - tion is ___ his re - ward. ___ To him, ___

life is a great big bang up. When - ev - er there's a

hang up, you'll find the Spi - der Man.

POKÉMON THEME

Theme to the English adapted anime series POKÉMON

Words and Music by T. LOEFFLER
and J. SIEGLER

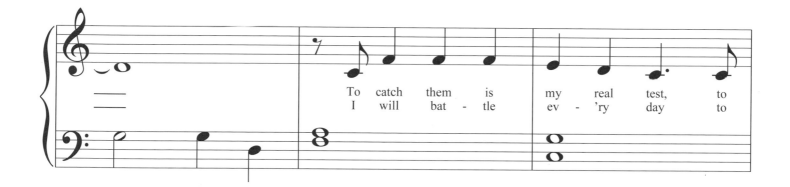

each Po - ké - mon to un - der - stand the pow - er that's ___ in - side. ___
Arm in arm we'll win the fight. It's al - ways been ___ our dream. ___

Po - ké - mon! Got - ta catch 'em all! It's you and ___ me.

I know it's my des - ti - ny. Po - ké - mon! Oh, you're

my best friend in a world we must ___ de - fend. ___ Po - ké - mon!

ROCKY & BULLWINKLE

from the Cartoon Television Series

Words and Music by
FRANK G. COMSTOCK

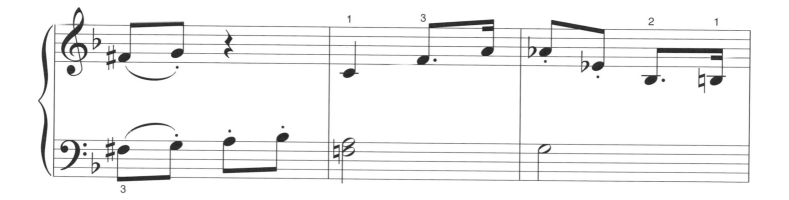

SPONGEBOB SQUAREPANTS THEME SONG

from SPONGEBOB SQUAREPANTS

Words and Music by MARK HARRISON,
BLAISE SMITH, STEVE HILLENBURG
and DEREK DRYMON

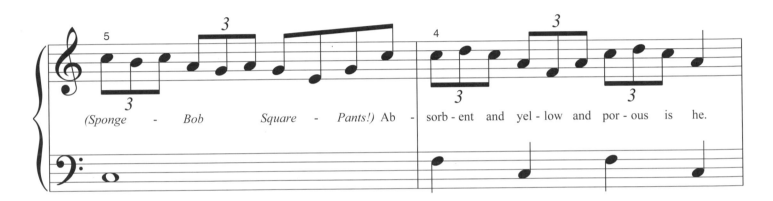

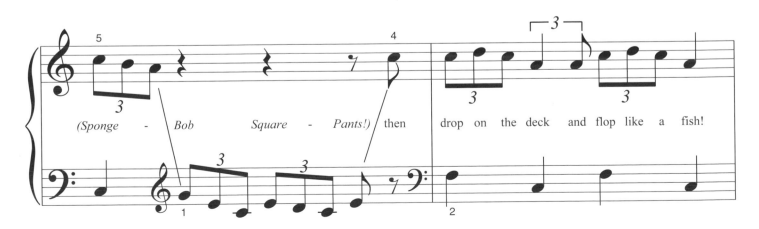

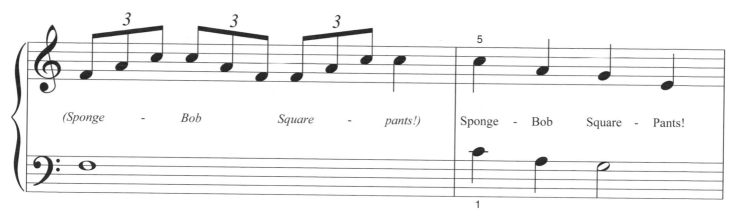

(Sponge - Bob Square - pants!) Sponge - Bob Square - Pants!

Sponge - Bob Square - Pants! Sponge - Bob Square - Pants!

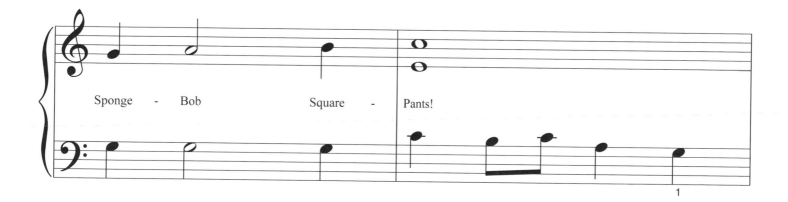

Sponge - Bob Square - Pants!

THOMAS THE TANK ENGINE
(Main Title)
from THOMAS THE TANK ENGINE

Words and Music by
ED WELCH

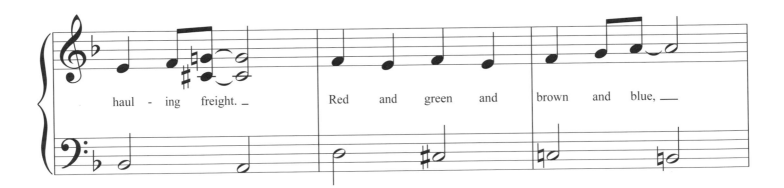

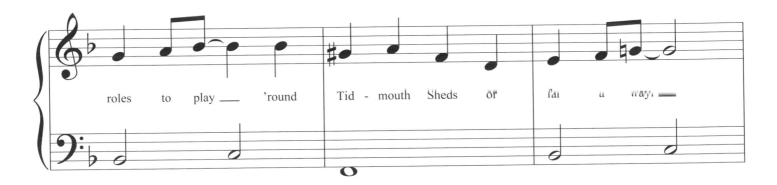

Down the hills and 'round the bends, — Thom - as and his

friends. Thom - as, he's the cheek - y one. __

James, he's vain, but lots of fun. __ Per - cy pulls the

mail on time. __ Gor - don thun - ders down the line. __

Em - i - ly real - ly knows her stuff. ___ Hen - ry toots and

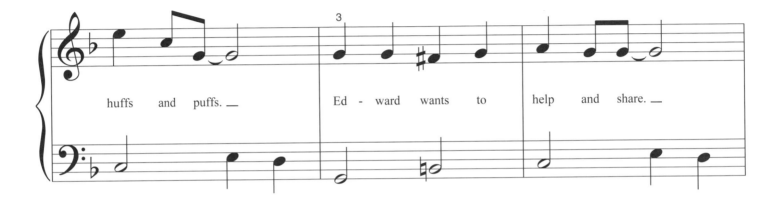

huffs and puffs. ___ Ed - ward wants to help and share. ___

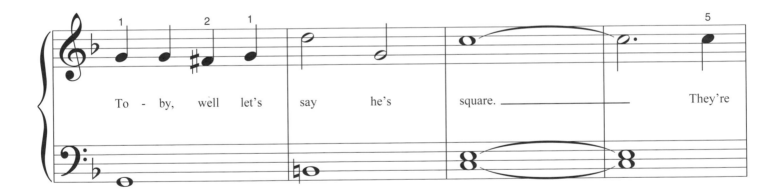

To - by, well let's say he's square. ___ They're

two, they're four, they're six, they're eight, ___ shunt - ing trucks and haul - ing freight. ___

Red and green and brown and blue, — they're the Real - ly Use - ful crew. —

All with diff - 'rent roles to play — 'round Tid - mouth Sheds or

far a - way. — Down the hills and 'round the bends, —

Thom - as and his friends. _____

WALLACE AND GROMIT THEME

from WALLACE AND GROMIT

By JULIAN NOTT

March tempo

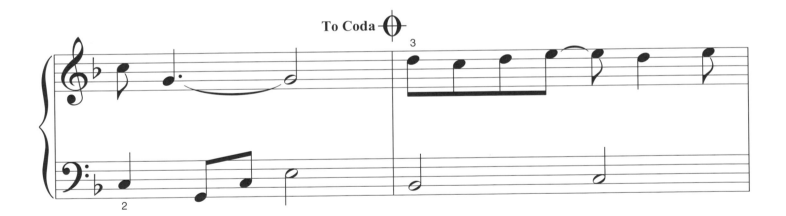

D.C. al Coda

CODA